What's

In

Your

Name?

THE SPIRITUAL SCIENCE OF NUMBERS
IN YOUR NAME AND HOW THEY AFFECT YOUR LIFE

Clifford W. Cheasley

ISBN 1-56459-402-5

CONTENTS

CHAPTER I

VIBRATION AND LIFE

LIFE and Vibration are synonymous terms —to interpret the latter is to comprehend the former.

To study the practical interpretation of vibration is to know the way of life, to unfold completely the mystery of the Self and to recognize how inter-related we humans are with every other plane of life that exists.

To possess this knowledge is becoming the object of all thinking people who realize that as the vibratory rate of our Universe increases, its inhabitants will naturally seek wisdom by which they may include life's lessons by the more rapid way of transmutation instead of the long, tiresome path of experience.

The majority of the world, of course, still lives unconsciously, faces its initiations in ignorance of them and of itself, depending upon intuitional faculties and spiritual guidance which its mentality cannot easily accept or prove, to make the pathway easier.

This majority is becoming less year by year, for many individuals, having discovered that life in its fundamental principle is divine law or God—order—are finding their place in the scheme of things and working from within outward, are learning the life of order and expression rather than of chaos and repression.

Life thus understood is simple, but misunderstood is a serious accident.

Daily, men and women risk honor, home, position and happiness upon an intuition or sometimes an impulse which they would be ashamed to follow in the management of their everyday life, their offices or their households.

In the latter expressions they have learned to be systematic by application of the law of mathematical precision, but in the former, where sentiment and the deeper human associations may be involved, they have only worm-eaten platitudes and Universal standards of right and wrong upon which to rely which never have and never will convince or corner that " I am " quality within us all which seeks for expression through our action, even though the results warned against may really come to pass.

Living in the material Universe and expressing our vibrations or life through the physical, it is only through a physical demonstration of the truth of being that the mass mind will comprehend the manipulation of the more subjective laws of right and wrong.

It is this physical demonstration that Numerology supplies by its use of numbers in relation with everyday life.

The numbers themselves tell nothing, but there has always been grouped around them a great deal of esoteric wisdom, and many centuries before Christ they were used by the Masters and teachers of the race as physical demonstrators of hidden vital truth.

[8]

"Figures do not lie." One numerical equation is more convincing than one thousand words of advice which are often forgotten as quickly as the personality of their author; and a science that reduces human impulses, desires and actions to certain equations which mean the same thing wherever found does not lie, but voices eternal truth in language that even the most skeptical, willful individualist will accept because he must.

Does such understanding take the romance from life? Not in any way! It opens up instead new anticipations and certainties of happiness where often doubt and ignorance resulting in fear and worry have existed; it prolongs the helpful associations of the present; awakens the Universal soul of man by linking him in understanding with all other planes of life and draws his mind from the danger of immersion in the smaller personalities of the moment.

Numerology uses nine numerals, simply and directly to reveal to the many this wisdom which has been the possession of the few since the human race began, and that has enabled these few to transcend the limitation of human living through the understanding of man's relationship and adjustment with and to God—Life—Vibration, which is in all and through all.

Each plane of earthly expression has its distinct laws of evolution which have to be experienced and expressed by its units before they can appear on a higher plane of expression, just as the pupil passes from the lowest to the highest form at school. Man is this highest form of vibration in the earth currents and has included in his journey from the atomic to the human kingdom all the vibratory zones of the mineral, vegetable and animal, as witnessed by man's positive control of these planes and his power to subject their laws to his will.

In the human vibrations there are many divisions through which we all pass and repass toward that stage where we can be removed from earth and express in angelic consciousness to meet again a new vibratory law.

In our journey from the first stages of human unfoldment we have lived many lives in various colors and conditions and every condition of every life which we have passed through has been created by ourselves as the result of understanding included previously, just as we recognize and handle the situations which come up in our present life and of which we have had previous experience.

The result of our contact with these conditions has been included in our soul-wisdom and been rated as a finished initiation in our cosmic record—our baptismal name.

It is always the most interesting to study ourselves and this work will be mainly devoted to this phase of Numerology, explaining why we do certain things, why we neglect others, why certain expressions appeal to us, why others do not, our real purpose in life and many other things that can increase our happiness and usefulness.

It must not be overlooked however that this study can and does teach us to reveal accurately the expression of *everything* that exists.

To the younger generation Numerology supplies a need which has been prayed for by all its educators for many years, who have found that their chief difficulty has been that the young, inexperienced minds on the edge of life will not accept for their own guides well meaning words spoken from experience of another person. Fresh from their education, the study of mathematics and from the consideration of the definite proofs which they offer, they do not consider it ridiculous or impossible to have their own nature numbered and tabbed and numbered sign-posts of danger pointed out to them along the road they are to travel, because it is language they understand.

To those who are well along life's pathway Numerology comes as a healing influence of revelation, answering the many whys and wherefores, turning the interrogation marks of uncertainty into exclamation points of certainty and conviction.

It points a way to take advantage of existing opportunities so that increased and lasting usefulness may be attained, and, what is more valuable very often, a method by which the experiences of the past can be transmuted into "stepping stones to higher things" for the future.

CHAPTER II

THE NUMBERS

THE numbers 1, 2, 3, 4, 5, 6, 7, 8, 9 go to make up a complete cycle of human initiation; and these numbers when fully understood can explain to us every expression that is possible in the material Universe, whether upon the mineral, vegetable, animal or human plane.

Each one of these numbers existing as a Universal cosmic force is neither constructive or destructive, as all vibration or life having originated from the One source of God-Creation is good; but they do express the forces explained under the head of " General Characteristics " appearing later in this chapter.

Therefore it is well to dispel from our minds the belief in "bad " or unlucky numbers for they are all good and lucky in themselves, and if we know enough about them we can choose to keep those around us which more particularly harmonize with our own vibrations, bringing ourselves always into relationships where our happiness lies.

It will be seen that the 1 to 9 cycle includes odd and even numbers and one of the first fundamentals which we can take into our understanding is that the former vibrate harmoniously to the intuitional, feminine or receptive expressions and the even numbers to the intellectual, masculine, side of life.

Beyond the general force of each vibration already mentioned there is constructive, destructive and negative action, but these are developed by the life spark in every expression manifesting, according to conscious or unconscious choice, the power of individual creation.

Man being the highest inclusion of vibratory law upon this material Universe has the power to develop the vibration or life principle of all the other earth planes into constructive or destructive action. This law is seen in the expression of two individuals who will bend to their wills the resources of one plane of life in entirely opposite directions.

Constructive action of any plane is just what its name implies: unfolding and evolving into higher usefulness. Destructive action is tearing down and destroying existing expression and through the neglect of reconstruction leaving an open doorway for entrance of the third aspect—negativity.

This last named aspect is that of force present but unexpressed corresponding on all planes to the darkness and formlessness of the Universe before the " spirit of God moved upon the face of the waters."

It explains the human expressions in whom we can discover high points of vibration, but who are occupying positions or born into families where their possibilities are repressed rather than unfolded.

When individuals grow weary of situations which do not really express them and hold day by day before their inner consciousness the vision of the situations that do as achievements that are not impossible to them, they are re-creating themselves back into the constructive expression of their vibrations; whereas, through condemnation and resistance they surround themselves with destructive action, just as by passivity and complete acceptance they can remain in the negative or stage of repression.

There is but an hair's breadth that divides the constructive from the destructive; and this is so often spanned unconsciously by the individual who, not really destructively inclined, finds so many methods of expression that have proved successful for his own life that he unconsciously forces these upon his neighbors and upon those who are under his charge, without consideration for the individual development of others, from which it is a short step to the continued destruction of the freedom of others and the destruction of his own personal opportunities, owing to the avoidance of his company by other of his fellows who represent vibrations which could very well complement his own and unfold his higher capabilities.

Thus we have General Characteristics for each vibration of 1 to 9. The General Characteristics are seen in action whether a vibration has been extended into the constructive, destructive or negative aspects.

We have also constructive action, which is the extending of individual vibration into the highest expression; destructive action, which is the misuse of man's divine power of creation, and negative action, which results from previous destructive action, but is the plane where through repressed conditions man is often forced to choose which he will serve and to build for constructive future.

GENERAL CHARACTERISTICS

1. *Creation.*—All life or vibration commenced with the 1 and therefore where this number is found it stands for personal creation and the building of individuality. It means individualization, self-assertiveness, self-reliance, reasoning and the faculties of the pioneer.

It cannot be expressed through too close attachment to individuals and conditions because it is the law of discards and means constant unity with conditions of adjustment, extracting material for building higher.

2. *Collection.*—The vibration of the mixer; collection of experiences, reflective rather than creative; the peacemaker; the base upon which broader material expressions are built up; responsible for the finest, smallest detail the " bricks " of all constructions.

3. *Personal Expression.* — Self-expres-

sion; adornment; art; criticism; observation. The composite of 1 and 2 has therefore added to the 1 of personal creation the experiences of the 2. Ambition; entertainment; social expression; fashion; inspiration; individual work.

This vibration is always necessary to the vibrations of 1 and 2, giving them complete expression, and is of itself more or less incomplete without either or both of these vibrations to rely on as an anchor or basis.

4. *Materiality.*—Lack of inspiration; home; patriotism; fact; endurance; application; concentration; positiveness; practicality; successful wage-earner. This vibration makes the understanding of spiritual and inspirational subjects difficult and gives dislike of social trivialities.

5. *Life Experience.*—This is a vibration that Pythagoras himself did not really understand and upon which modern interpreters have little to say.

It is the extension into a new cycle of expression and stands for dislike of control; eager interest in life and living; investigation; research into metaphysical subjects; inspiration; optimism; variety; science; versatility; companionship; originality; ease; fascination. This vibration gives attraction to everything but is held by nothing and is untrammeled in its choice of many phases of life expression.

6. *Cosmic Adjustment.*—Home; friendship; respectability; responsibility; care of individuals; reliability; domesticity; action; conscientiousness; attachment; morality; hospitality. It is the vibration that is drawn to marriage as an institution and that without personal responsibility through the care of other people will attach itself to care for pets; is the vibration of cosmic motherhood.

7. *Subjective Re-arrangement.*—The vibration of the finished worker; rest; peace; alone-ness; reflection; worship; reticence; this vibration is drawn to dim lights, soft colors, all nature's expressions and to be rather jealous of its private life.

8. *Material Perfection.*—This vibration is the compositive of 2, 4, which gives its supremacy upon the material planes. It gives competence in all commercial or material problems; judgment; justice; research into spiritual things; dissatisfaction with limited material conditions; direction; control; organization.

9. *Complete Expression.* — Intuition; deeper human understanding; emotion; sympathy; the extremist; freedom in action and thought; unorthodox; philanthropy; socialism; disregard of possessions; drama; tragedy; music; art.

In the conjunction of 3, 6 and 9 we have the complete trinity of artistic vibration. 3 the finer detailed decoration and the art of personal expression and adornment; 6 home arrangement and decoration; and 9 the expression of the soul of art in all directions.

CHAPTER III

WHAT THE NAME MEANS

"WHAT'S in a name?" is an expression that we often hear spoken carelessly without being able to supply a convincing answer. It is this answer that NUMEROLOGY supplies by interpreting the true characteristics in the expression of everything that lays claim to possess a name which is its own and by which it is recognized among men.

In the name of anything we have simply the vowels and consonants from which to adjudge its vibrations.

The value of the consonants, the shell of a language, was first discovered by Dr. Julia Seton, founder of the New Thought Church and School (Church of the New Civilization), who recognizes that the consonants decide the personality of the individual or thing under consideration.

NUMEROLOGY dealing with individuals in character analyzation deals with the baptismal name—that is, all the Christian names and surname which you received at baptism, or, if you were not baptized, those which you were given by your parents or guardians. It interprets the character from three distinct standpoints called respectively: "IDEALITY," "IMPRESSION" and "EXPRESSION."

The vibration of the first is found from the simple addition of all the vowels in your name, the second is found from the addition of all the consonants and the third and last, from the addition of both the vowels and consonants.

"Addition" does not mean the adding up of the number of vowels, and consonants that appear, but in adding the numbers which will appear under each letter of your name after you have conformed to the

[19]

following rules given in "Casting the name for analysis."

First, however, it is necessary to fully understand what the terms IDEALITY, IMPRESSION and EXPRESSION mean.

It is well known that there is a great difference between what an individual may look like in his personality, how he may conduct himself in every-day expression and what he really is if we could get a glimpse of the real inner nature. This is the difference between IDEALITY, IMPRESSION and EXPRESSION.

Ideality reveals the character of our inner nature or what we are, Impression tells what we look like through the vibration of our personality, and Expression tells the channels which we choose to express ourselves by in our daily contact with life.

Our name is an exact record of our place in the cosmic plan; it is not an accident but a vibratory structure which we ourselves have built somewhere, have created, experienced and are now come to express.

[20]

Casting a Name for Analysis.—The following is the chart of Pythagoras vibratory cycle of 1 to 9 and the alphabet arranged into nine divisions.

A	B	C	D	E	F	G	H	I
J	K	L	M	N	O	P	Q	R
S	T	U	V	W	X	Y	Z	
1	2	3	4	5	6	7	8	9

The following example of preparing a name is the clearest method of applying these numbers and will afford the utmost ease in reading the character of a name after it has been practised a few times.

$$
\begin{array}{l}
\quad\quad\quad\quad\;\; 5 \;\; + \;\; 5 \;\; + \;\; 3 \;\; + \;\; 9 = 22 = 4 \quad \text{IDEALITY} \\
\text{S Y L V E S T E R C U R T I S S} \\
1{+}7{+}3{+}4 \;+\; 1{+}2 \;+\; 9 \;\;\; 3 \;+\; 9{+}2 \;+\; 1{+}1 = 43 = 4{+}3 = 7 \\
\quad\quad\quad\quad\quad\quad\quad\quad\quad\quad\quad\quad\quad\quad\quad \text{IMPRESSION}
\end{array}
$$

$$
\begin{array}{l}
\text{S Y L V E S T E R C U R T I S S} \\
1{+}7{+}3{+}4{+}5{+}1{+}2{+}5{+}9 \;+\; 3{+}3{+}9{+}2{+}9{+}1{+}1 = 65 = 6{+}5 = 11 = \\
\quad\quad\quad\quad\quad\quad\quad\quad\quad\quad\quad\quad\quad 1{+}1 = 2 = \text{EXPRESSION}
\end{array}
$$

In this example we have first dealt with the vowels in the name, placing over the top of each the number that corresponds to it in the table given. We have added the numbers thus given together until we have obtained a single digit, which has given us the Ideality.

The Ideality we have seen tells the basis of the character, the real strength of our inner ideals and desires; what we really are, as distinct from anything that we may appear to be. When a person's everyday expression, for instance, is interrupted by adverse circumstances the vibration which is relied upon for new inspiration to rise is that of the Ideality. It depends therefore upon this vibration, whether the individual is really ambitious, religious, material or inspirational in the heart of his composition, and when we see any individual doing a big work in life, it tells us just how true this expression is to the real ideal of the individual or the motive that prompts its continuance.

When the Ideality has been found, turn to its number in Chapter Five, remembering always that, dealing with the Ideality, the explanations given will correspond to the inner ideals or what it is desired to express, and should be prefaced with the sentence, " You desire to be."

Referring again to the name we have cast, we see that the consonants were the next to be dealt with, and that, dealing with each consonant, we found at last a final digit, 7, which told us the Impression. Turning to the explanations of the numbers again will tell us the characteristics which this individual would look as if he possessed.

A final reference to the second casting of the name shows that both the vowels and the consonants were added together until the final digit of 2 was obtained.

Reference to number 2 in our explanations will tell what this individual really expresses in everyday life.

CHAPTER IV

CONSTRUCTION OR DESTRUCTION

It has always been a point in the interpretation of character by number vibration, how it is possible to tell whether an individual has developed himself constructively to conform to the constructive side of the vibration of his " Expression " or whether he is living upon the destructive and is misapplying his possibilities.

Numerology is the only science of self-analysis that can read the character and ability accurately without the subject being known or seen by the interpreter; and as such, it is finding a valuable place in the world because of the fact that the distance between the reader and the subject is of no account, providing the full baptismal name can be obtained.

Recent revelations through the mind of the author have disclosed a simple law which also makes the decision as to constructive and destructive action just as easy.

In the first place, a study of vibration can only lead to one conclusion as regards the two expressions, one of which the world upholds as " good " and the other which it condemns and often shuns as " bad."

This conclusion is that if all life is the expression of certain vibrations and these vibrations are all rays of the One divine source of creation, all expression is good; but that the greater number of times a certain number appears in the name which is the vibratory chart of an individual, the greater intensification shall we see of the action for which this number stands.

This leads us to understand that what is called constructive action is where one vibration balances or restrains another; and what is called destructive action or " bad " is sure to occur where all vibration is on the one scale and has no natural restraining influences from the direction of its fellows which are the weaker in proportion.

It is not difficult with this understanding to discover that lack of balance makes a criminal or produces an enemy to society. Environment, although an aid, is never all to blame or there would be no persons who through some quality within themselves have transcended its limitations.

The cause lies in the fact that any individual, with an uneven balance of vibration, which the simple law of mathematics will decide as accurately as the chemist separates and labels his qualities and quantities, sent out into life with entire ignorance of himself and of where this lack of balance will lead, is certain to express destructively in any environment in which he may find himself.

This explanation has escaped all but a few of the world's inhabitants, because everyone is too occupied looking at, talking about, and endeavoring to eliminate effects, to use enough commonsense to search for the cause, and in many cases attempting to protect themselves and the members of their families from these very effects expressed through other people, when within themselves and the units of their own circle causes are unconsciously being set in motion which can and will produce as dire results.

Understanding is the only antidote for temptation and violation, and when the guardians of the child and those great souls who are giving their lives in a worthy effort to restrain the effects of impulses and seek thereby to uplift the race will commence to understand that all life is mathematical and subject to the divine law of order they will have in their hands an instrument which they can wield far more powerfully than all the wealth in all the banks of the world which they would now apply to correction, discipline or example.

The youth of our race is not led astray

unless there is that weakness in the individual law of vibration which makes following easy; and the only method of preventing contamination in any class is to see that where the weakness is discovered its possessor is made aware of it before its effect is shown, so that he or she, understanding its possibilities, can arm and be armed effectively against temptation.

The first and principal method of applying this law to individuals is to compare the digits of " Ideality " and " Expression." Should the same number appear in both cases, destructive action in the Expression number or both is assumed; should one number be even and the other odd, constructive action of the " Expression " number is assured by the fairly even balance that is obtained.

For example, we will take the Idealities and Expressions of two individuals, in the first: Ideality 9, Expression 8; and in the second: Ideality 5 and Expression 5.

This illustration will prove the law of

balance which only numbers can determine for the individual where even expression has not appeared.

The first example cannot follow the destructive action of his odd Ideality 9, which is his desire for self-indulgence, and attraction to emotion, passion, hate and selfishness, because his even number of 8 Expression is opposite and demands perfection and ideal expression upon the material plane; neither can he express through the destructive side of his 8 Expression which is injustice and oppression, because of the restraint that is exercised by the humanitarian and sympathetic qualities of his 9 Ideality.

Our second example having the identical vibration in the two most important equations of his character can be just as expressed in the destructive side of this vibration of 5, which is sex, appetite and self-indulgence, as his training and opportunity may allow.

The individual who is living up to the

constructive explanation of his name vibration is on the path of destiny; while he who answers to the destructive aspect is building fate or " karma " for the future which will cause his expression sometime, somewhere in the negative aspect.

Those who come by this knowledge may profit by it, and by the knowledge of their own vibrations of Ideality and Expression and the comparison of their expression of them with the explanations that follow can adjust themselves constructively into Universal harmony.

The standards of one vibration must never be compared with the standards of another, for they are all distinct processes of initiation governed by their own law, and necessary steps to their neighbors.

CHAPTER V

NUMBERS IN ACTION

1. *Constructive Expression* — INDIVIDUALIZATION. You are conscious of your own importance but not blind to the rights of others nor inconsiderate of their opinions. You ask the advice of other people but use this advice only as an aid to your own opinion, which is, and should always be, dictated by a feeling of confidence in your own expressions. You choose freely from the things around you what you need for a more perfect expression of your individuality, do not hang on to any expression of individual or situation too long, but discard readily the things that you have outgrown in order that you can pass on to higher and more developed possibilities. You love and give without thought of return and make willing unity with all con-

ditions without resistance or self-pity for the expressions that you are called upon to surrender.

Destructive Expression — DOMINANCE. You are egotistical, inconsiderate of other people's expressions because you are so close to the personality of your own expression. You are given to living other people's lives for them by recommending methods which *you* have found perfect, instead of minding your own business. You worry and plan too much about the conditions around your life instead of showing the more universal spirit of trust and faith and letting your mind soar free of circumstances. You seek to hold individuals and conditions to your own personal life and surrender them only with a good deal of resistance, self-pity and remorse. You give advice where it is not asked and are given to studying the position and prospects of individuals rather than their feelings. You are " I," " I," " I " all through life.

2. *Constructive Expression* — DIPLO-MACY. You are tactful, anxious to please, never aggressive, but rather wait for the opinions of others before expressing your own. You show yourself willing to learn and collect all the knowledge on all the subjects you hear of, and to mix freely and upon an apparent basis of equality with all kinds and conditions of your fellow beings. You can place yourself readily under the law of giving and receiving by rendering the smallest service where asked. You will make any effort for peace and will always act as the peacemaker, seeking to appease the anger of others, and keeping your own temper in some trying circumstances.

You are individualized, but your individuality, gained in the initiation of the 1 vibration, is always kept in the background and is only expressed in a persistent way and never dominantly.

The Destructive Expression—INDIFFERENCE. You are rather disgruntled, easily roused to anger; can become wilfully destructive, tearing and destroying simply for the pleasure that destruction affords you. You do not care to mix and have no great development of individuality. You are careless of your surroundings, the people you mix with, and your appearance, and will abide only by the standards which you set for yourself from time to time. You make all kinds of promises but seldom fulfil any of them.

3. *Constructive Expression*—AMBITION. You take every opportunity that is offered for increasing your self-expression though always remembering the principle of concentration and order in your expressions and researches. You are sociable, willing to entertain without making yourself a spectacle through your self-expression. You strive to be the last word in the expression of your personality through being well dressed and artistic in your choice of dress and surroundings. You are inspirational, not seeking work with your hands

[34]

but rather in the artistic or expressive zones. You like to be an interesting companion to others and are always tolerant of other people's errors even while you see these very quickly. You can show patience in waiting for the materialization of your creations and in dealing with other people.

The Destructive Expression—INTOLERANCE. You are rather selfish and have not a very high principle and are not above taking any means to get what you want or to attain your ambition of perfected personal expression. You are not serious enough to perfect yourself fully in any accomplishment, but following the latest attraction are rather unconcentrated, not really knowing what you want or how to get it. You are exacting and critical, engaged in an endless comparison of your own expression with that of others and always disparage yourself. You are impatient, feather-brained, and always know how everything should be done and said

[35]

and it is difficult for other people to tell you anything.

4. *Constructive Expression* — STEADFASTNESS. You are governed by your intellect and reason. You pay close attention to detail work in life and the working methods of the subjects and objects which you meet. You are seeking to raise yourself by a higher perfection in technicality; you are ambitious for knowledge of the practical useful kind and to rise to a position of power. You are willing to work, and study hard to achieve and can be very painstaking. You are not interested in spiritual or intuitional subjects unless they can show practical demonstrations, and will not rebel against legitimate control exerted over you by other individuals or against the expression of service in your own life. You are very honest, reliable and exact, practical and can obey orders.

Destructive Expression — DISCONTENT. You are dissatisfied with service, always consider that you are being exploited by other people, a clock-watcher and servant only because you have to employ your time somehow. You aspire to the higher places of control but will not work to prepare yourself for them. You are as good as everyone else in your own estimation and always likely to cause dissatisfaction to yourself and others. You pooh! pooh! everything that you cannot see the reason of at first glance and prevent others from seeking further along lines which you have rejected.

5. *Constructive Expression*—NEW LIFE. You are inspirational, inventive and intuitional; personally free, a traveler, a welcome companion, meeting life with open arms, ready to make unity with every experience that you meet as a means for higher unfoldment and expansion of yourself. You endeavor to maintain a Christ-like expression by your universal attitude to conditions and through your versatility; yet you know what you want without needing to plan and prepare for your goal.

You rely more upon the unexpected rather than anticipate results and through faith and confidence in your own quality of expression are optimistic, fascinating, inspiring to others, expressing sympathy with other people's troubles and courage in your own. You live to your ideals and develop something in your life along scientific lines which can be a new interest to you continually, providing you with the opportunity to uplift others.

Destructive Expression — INDULGENCE. You express through self-indulgence in sex, appetite and self. You are very uncertain in your vibration, being very changeable in your actions. You have rather a poor moral standard and yet carry off your actions with a good deal of bravado which disarms many who would otherwise condemn. You procrastinate, are not a very good investment as an employee or friend, as you cannot be depended upon to make good in service or promises, although you are always full of ideas which gain people's confidence. You resist change in the circumstances of your own personal life unless change is a matter of your own desire, and destroy your opportunities by holding on too long to things in a very similar way to the 1 vibration.

6. *Constructive Expression*—RELIABILITY. You are a comforter giving willing service. You are conscientious, maintaining your own individuality even in service. You have a great love of home and friends and family and do not wish to live alone, nor for yourself alone, always expressing cheerfulness, never despondent, always the busy finisher of what you undertake even though it is not always easy to you. You are satisfied with pleasure in a quiet way and are rather a restful and cheering influence.

Destructive Expression—ANXIETY. You are too anxious to serve even when and where you are not wanted. You overburden your life by the things that you voluntarily take on to do for others and

[89]

are not such a restful influence, as you are given to bustle and to interfere and unable to stop for rest or relaxation. You sink your individuality in service, often likely to become anchored to some life whose thoughts and acts you will find yourself copying to the destruction of your own individuality. You are imposed upon by others and resent it without seeing the cause.

7. *Constructive Expression*—PLACIDITY. You are calm, refined and studious. You do not seek for constant expression in objective things, but ask only the opportunity to give something to the world as a priest would give it. You do not seek to control business or finance which do not interest you, but seek to develop something in your own life which can attract supply to you by its worth. You are engaged in work that takes you away from the bustle and noise of commerce where you have more opportunity to express in your own way, and from " behind the scenes " as it were,

the truths which you feel subjectively. Having to spend much time alone you are not lonely, for through your attention to worship and introspection you can easily find many interests. You do not condemn expressions which you do not understand, but contact all life with an open mind. You are a worshiper, a listener rather than a talker, making every experience of life and individuals develop your subjective nature and provide new food for thought and theory.

The Destructive Expression—TURBULENCE. You are rather difficult to live with as you are very individualized and endeavor to make other people conform to your rather peculiar methods of expression. You condemn the things that do not conform with your theories and imagine that you have more ability than you really have in the objective world of business and seek to control, direct and dictate, material policy. You are rather unreasonable, not able to rest or live away from city life for long at a time and always being annoyed by its inconveniences when you have to unite with it.

8. *Constructive Expression* — JUSTICE. You are successful in commercial expression and organization, take a personal interest as far as possible in all those you find around you as employees or helps, and while using these individuals legitimately to attain your own success you endeavor at the same time to give them the best opportunity of perfecting their own expression. You are very even tempered, with a good balance of intuition and intellect, although more inclined to be led by the latter. You have material freedom, direction and control; and financial aid will always come to supply your needs.

Destructive Expression — INJUSTICE. You are successful in direction and control but destructive in your use of power, sweating those under you and taking the rôle of the oppressor and bully if you can serve your own ends. You seek to keep every other person connected with you subject to your individuality and never co-operate, only command. You are unscrupulous in your efforts to obtain and maintain your personal material freedom. Your main ideal in life is to have a greater expression of finance than anyone else because of the control that this can give you.

9. *Constructive Expression* — Love. You are humanitarian, a philanthropist, regarding all people of whatever race, color or creed as your brothers; having the highest expression of impersonal love, sending out, in your contact with others, only love, justice, mercy, seeking to make every man your friend. You exercise the power of healing consciously and unconsciously by speaking the right word at the right time and helping people in their troubles, relying upon your intuitional faculty more than the intellectual reason to guide you. Realizing your power over all other human expressions, you seek to use this influence constructively, standing as a revelator

[43]

through art, through the power of healing or as a counsellor, giving willing service to humanity, and have learned to transmute all passions into love and all personal desire into Universal understanding. You are free to go where you will and welcomed by everyone. You do not care for personal possessions and give freely of your substance, material and inspirational, to help the world to more complete expression.

Destructive Expression—DESIRE. You are rather personal in your expressions and desires, making distinctions between classes of human beings which extend far past their ordinary expressions. You use destructively to gain your own ends and for your own self-satisfaction the power which you have over the human emotions, by taking advantage of the confidences you gain from others in business, love or friendship. You play upon the emotions of your own and other's compositions because of the fascinating interest which this affords and can easily express in anger, violent and blasting passions and personal love and raise these in others at will. In this expression you use the power of dramatic speech and emotional expression destructively and know how to wound by your words as no other vibration does, biting in your sarcasm, aggravating and passionate.

This is the most destructive expression even according to Universal standards, for in it homes are laid desolate, hearts broken, trusts betrayed and individuals' lives surrounded with dead ashes of memory and physical wastes of disease.

NOTE—It is more usual to find in the interpretation of character by numbers, that individuals correspond to a few constructive and a few destructive explanations and the author's intention is that by being acquainted with the two possibilities of our own vibrations we can readily tell when in our everyday expression we cross the line between them.

CHAPTER VI

NEGATIVE ACTION

As the explanations given below are followed it will not be difficult to interpret the expressions of many individuals whom one meets continually in a day's living and is rather at a loss to understand the purpose of their life.

The man who shines your shoes, the woman who scrubs your floors may both be above the plane upon which they are living, possessed of powerful vibrations which, although sensed by us through the indications of their personality, are to them as yet unknown and undiscovered in this incarnation.

Again, this aspect of vibration explains the artist born into an inartistic family; the individuals who are entitled by the quality of their vibration to material free-

dom and yet living in circumstances where
to obtain the cost of every meal is a strug-
gle. It is the explanation that so many
wonderful constructive mental inspirational
and material creations are born from the
minds of those who are kept to an invalid
chair for the better part of their lives.

The physical limitation upon all planes
is the negative inaction which is the pay-
ment for former destructive living out of
vibration; but here the higher self is often
doubly awake to the constructive possibilities of life and reveals these possibilities
to others by wonderful transcended expressions of the mind. The quality of such
expression has been so intensified in many
cases that the individuals have transmuted
the physical limitation of the present life
and become once more four-square with
expression of body and spirit. In this
action of the law of vibration the world
sees a miracle of healing, its newspapers
write of the circumstances, but the individual knows only, that prayers, visions

[47]

and constructive building have come to expression.

Everyone in any stage of negativity is given this chance to work back into constructive expression and to regain the inheritance which they have forfeited sometime, somewhere.

1. *Limitation.*—Individuals who have little backbone in life, ready to perform the meanest service. Often seen as those people who one is certain could do higher work in life than what they are engaged in, if they could only be raised to a consciousness of themselves. Victims of their own destructive law in the past, these individuals are very often seen as blind, deaf or afflicted in some way, where they have never had an opportunity in this life to assert individuality or to be self-reliant, but have always been dependent upon others.

2. *Dependence.*—Lacks the force to gain very much for itself. Has very few individual opinions and readily reflects the

ideas and expressions of the people around it. Is too easily persuaded into doing meaner work for other people; is seldom contented but feels the burden of life and living rather heavily. While it is not disgruntled, does not feel the urge to mix with others.

3. *Repression.*—Will not or cannot take advantage of the opportunities offered to express the self, in artistic or any other lines. Unconcentrated; undecided, cannot make up their mind to any one expression, but taking up many things, doing a little of one and a little of another. Victims of their own destructive law in the past, are seen with the desire to express, but in an environment where accomplishment and higher development is impossible to them; led by circumstances to engage in unsuitable, technical work.

4. *Lack of Ambition.*—Just mechanical workers, working because they have to live and not for their personal advancement in any way. Not a very high development of

[49]

intellect, asking only the opportunity to work and live from day to day.

5. *Crucifixion.*—Always seen to be fighting some little "fox in the vines" or some subtle craving for self-indulgence which it is hard to rise above. Has a good deal of surrender of the things which it values most, many times because of the little indulgences which it lacks the strength of itself to overcome. Financial loss and negation to include. These individuals are often pictures of their destructive self-indulgence of the past, through devitalized bodies, disease and deformity.

6. *Inhospitality.*—Unwilling to serve; refuses responsibility through the care of individuals and situations. Is not so eager to associate, but more given to live alone in perfect detachment from other people. Rather despondent, tired through service, leaving other people and conditions to take care of themselves.

7. *Misunderstanding.*—Feel always unable to express anything that they feel in

their inner nature, consider that no one wants them or understands them, and that they have never had a chance. Victims of their destructive law in the past, are seen to be surrounded with many responsibilities and relationships from which they find it hard to be free, and which prevent them from gaining that opportunity to be alone which is so necessary to their unfoldment.

8. *Failure.*—Unsuccessful in speculation. Find it difficult to gain the prestige which they feel themselves capable of, in the business world. Victims of their destructive law of the past, are seen to be born into a family and to live in an environment where there is lack of material expression instead of freedom, where money is scarce and where they have to give the meaner expressions of service.

9. *Emotion.*—Full of contradictory vibrations; too easily moved by the things that appeal to the emotional nature. Undermine their expression by being over generous and take the troubles of others

to themselves, weeping with those that weep, giving to all who ask, even beggaring themselves. Have lost the power of using other people either for good or bad, and are imposed upon by others freely. Unable to obtain much for themselves as they are torn this way and that by the force of their own vibrations.

CHAPTER VII

WHAT THE BIRTH DATE INDICATES

As in Astrology, the date of a person's birth plays a very important part in character delineation by Numerology.

The baptismal Name of an individual tells what the soul has included in the past and what it is qualified to express in the present, but the vibrations of the day, month and year of birth, indicate what has next to be included.

The Number gained by the addition of the vibrations of the birth date denotes exactly the initiation which it is to the individual's highest good to include in harmonious adjustment. It undoubtedly constitutes the greatest attracting force of a life, being responsible, as it is, for the conditions among which the person finds

himself from time to time. It attracts the
cities and countries in which he lives, his
companions and positions, and shows
clearly the possibility there is of expressing
himself in the way he desires and of attain-
ing his ideals. Whatever forces are shown
on the PATH OF LIFE as the vibrations of
birth are called, will have to be met and
included whether harmoniously or otherwise, for they constitute the inclusion of
certain lessons which the soul wishes to
express in a future life.

The method for determining the vibration of the Path of Life is very simple—
the calendar number of the month is placed
underneath whichever month opens the
date of birth, this is followed by the addition of the numbers in the day and in
the year, as follows:

$$\text{August} \quad 2+8 \quad 1+8+9+1 = \text{Aug. 28, 1891}$$
$$8 \quad + \quad 1+0+ \quad 1+9 = 19 = 10 = 1 \text{ PATH OF LIFE}$$

To aid one to understand better what influence THE PATH OF LIFE will have upon
the expression of an individual, and whether

[54]

the life will be easy or difficult, Numerology compares it with the vibration of the EXPRESSION, and whenever we see this duplicated as the digit of the PATH OF LIFE, we may know that the individual will have little to contend with in life; for instance, an EXPRESSION 4, on a PATH OF LIFE vibrating 4, would not be expected to meet anything which could not be easily overcome, as, although it might meet some conflicting influences under the separate vibrations of the month, day and year of the birth date, it is strongly connected through life with its own force.

This is the path of Self-perfection where the soul has the opportunity to round off, as it were, the inclusion of a former lesson.

There are many individuals found with a PATH OF LIFE weaker in vibration than their EXPRESSION, and these people are always connected with expressions of life and people who are beneath them. Whatever they attain is the result of their own efforts and not of opportunities and privileges they meet in life. Their complaint is that they are withheld from the opportunities their soul desires; but did they but realize it, there is no force in their life strong enough to withhold them from anything, except that which they express from their own inclusion. They meet nothing stronger than themselves and are always prepared for emergencies.

This is the path of the teacher, revelator and messenger, rather than that of the student, and is the opportunity the soul takes to express centuries of inclusion.

Lastly, there is the individual whose PATH OF LIFE is found to be higher than the vibration of the EXPRESSION, and this life is always climbing to make itself equal with the many splendid opportunities it meets. This is the most difficult of the two PATHS OF LIFE, for the individual must always hug his ideals close to his heart and take care that there are no false steps. It is the path of experience, and gives influential friends, position and opportunity.

[56]

This PATH OF LIFE is the indication that
the soul has been true in the past, and as
a reward is given, in the present, new
worlds to conquer.

The golden rule for the harmonious inclusion of the lesson of the PATH OF LIFE
is *adjustment;* and in order to help us to
apply this law, we should understand that
it is the purpose of every individual only
to intensify the characteristics of the PATH
OF LIFE.

The essence of the lesson of each vibration with the corresponding " watchwords "
are as follows:

1. Creation   Watchword—UNITY
2. Construction   Watchword—SERVICE
3. Expression   Watchword—PEACE
4. Materiality   Watchword—SERVICE
5. Experience   Watchword—UNITY
                             through NON-RESISTANCE
6. Attachment   Watchword—LOVE and SERVICE
7. Subjective Development   Watchword—PEACE
8. Material Perfection   Watchword—SERVICE
9. Complete Expression   Watchword—UNIVERSAL
                                          LOVE

If the individual will find which of these
Numbers correspond with the vibration of

his PATH OF LIFE he has the principle and
its "watchword," which together form the
key to his happiness, and that which will
help him to understand how to overcome
by adjustment the obstacles he meets.

READING THE BIRTH DATE

In reading the Birth date, we take up
first the final digit, the number 1 in the
above case, and understand that this vibration and everything it means to us in our
explanations of the individual vibrations is
the main lesson which this life has come to
include.

Secondly, we divide roughly the Birth
date into three cycles of time, making the
calendar number of the month occupy the
first, the digit of the day the second and the
digit of the year the third, with the understanding that although the experiences indicated by all the numbers will follow the individual all through life, those coming under
the vibration of the month will be more evi-

dent until 25 years of age, those indicated by the day from 25 to 50 years, and those under the year for the remainder of the life.

It is thus possible to explain many of the initiations that we are meeting more strongly at the particular age in which we are expressing and enables us to come nearer to the understanding of our attitude to life than we have been able to do previously.

Finally, we find the essence of the Path of Life by finding its final digit in the table given and the watchword which is indicated as helping us to unfold its highest possibilities. Example.

```
August 2+8   1893
   8     1+0   2+1
   8  +   1  +   3  = 1 + 2 = 3 Path of Life.
 ⌣⌣⌣   ⌣⌣⌣   ⌣⌣⌣
25 years 25-50   50
```

When the Path of Life vibration has been dealt with thus, read the constructive explanation of its final digit, **3** in our example, prefacing the reading with the sentence, " you have come to learn to be "; read next the constructive explanation of the particular cycle number our life is in at the time of reading according to our present age. These explanations will be found in Chapter Five.

CHAPTER VIII

CHANGING THE NAME—SIGNA-TURES—CHOOSING NAMES

THE name which we receive at birth has been proved to be an exact indication to our character and our ability in this life. It has also been seen, however, that this name from the vibratory standpoint does not always relate us in the best possible attitude to the lessons we came to learn as shown from the PATH OF LIFE.

By changing our name, therefore, we adjust ourselves more favorably to the experiences which we are bound to meet in this life, giving ourselves a better chance of success. It is a revelation sometimes, if we will just glance over the " materials " at our disposal in this life and try to see whether we have used or are using them in a way that will enable us to build the

[61]

finest " house " according to the plan laid out over our PATH OF LIFE.

In choosing a new name for ourselves or in adjusting the one which we are already entitled to, there are several important but simple rules to be considered:

1. To choose a name that in its final digit is along the same zone, either odd or even, as our own name vibrations, i.e., if our own name is numbered upon the odd side to choose a signature with an odd digit.

2. To choose a name that in the individual digits is harmonious. Names that have a final digit made up of odd and even digits are not harmonious, such as $1 + 6 + 7 = 5$, as such an expression has to be put along two lines, odd and even, and there must be a separation of energy.

3. To choose a name that in its final digit is in the same zone, odd or even, as the PATH OF LIFE vibration, as this leads the life to development in the right direction.

[62]

The effect of changing the name and of signing a new signature is to bring around us different influences and conditions by intensifying in our life the force which is seen as its digit.

The use of a capable knowledge of how to change the name is of great far-reaching result, for it is often seen that in the signature is the explanation of certain conditions which are provoking us.

It is not advisable to advocate the wholesale changing of names for yourself or others after this knowledge is included, as all life is initiation and the signature intensifying certain experiences gives us undoubtedly certain initiations which cannot be ignorantly interrupted. There is one infallible indication that the signature should be changed and this is when its bearer is dissatisfied with its form, is unhappy under certain conditions and is willing, without knowing what will happen, to allow the signature to be changed. Such an individual is ready to be lifted out into new experiences.

The change of name only very slightly affects our Ideality, is more apparent in the change which it gives to our Impression and most of all is seen to affect our Expression, bringing out in our everyday life just the qualities which its vibration stands for: 1. Individuality and self-reliance. 2. Diplomacy and association. 3. Perfected personal Expression. 4. Technicality and attention to little material things. 5. Change and versatility. 6. Responsibilities, care of individuals. 7. Aloneness, reflection, misunderstanding in material things. 8. Direction and control, material freedom. 9. Generosity, emotion, art.

SIGNATURES

The signature of a stranger, upon a letter or elsewhere, can tell us quickly the characteristics which the individual is intensifying and the vibration through which he is attempting to gain a higher unfoldment for himself.

Consideration of the signature of a married woman determines the initiation which her marriage has placed her life under and will be found to explain the new experiences which have been included since its adoption.

The individual who will get the most accurate reading of the signature is the one who is given to intensify one way of signing the name, for where so many different signatures are used, the conditions of the life are more subject to change and less easy to determine as distinct experiences.

CHOOSING NAMES FOR CHILDREN

Naturally such a knowledge of vibration as NUMEROLOGY provides, will lead us on to the question of how to name our children, and in this extension there are some very interesting and definite findings.

Numerology does not advocate the choosing of the name of a child by a person outside of the parents, because it looks upon the consciousness of the child as simply an extension of the consciousness of its father and mother. Therefore, it believes that with the parents should rest the choice of a name and that this choice should be made according to harmony in sound. Tone is a much finer scheme of vibration than numbers, and if the sound of a name is harmonious to the parents of a child, that child and its name invariably possesses the characteristics of its parents, but in different relationship, and stands revealed to the one who understands human vibration, as a correct extension of the consciousness that attracted it.

When a child's name has been chosen in this way, one who understands the law can step in and by their knowledge explain along what lines the child should be developed, forecasting the experiences that it will meet.

This method of naming children is not indorsed in any other system as far as is known, because most teachers prefer to demonstrate their science by choosing the name according to their own individual idea of an harmonious name, forgetting that there is a danger of thus interfering with the experiences which the child may have come to get in this life. Seldom is it that any attempt is made either, to choose a name which contains the vibrations of the parents, and the neglect of this is the cause of great estrangement in the future, for the child develops out of harmony with its parents, even though it may be under the law of harmony according to abstract vibration.

It will be readily seen that this method of dealing with the names of children does not detract in any way from the usefulness of Numerology, but only insures the really correct choice of a name by the parties who, typifying the consciousness which attracted the ego, are most qualified to identify and extend themselves through its expression.

The name of the child should be chosen

before birth, as this has been proved to have the effect of causing the birthday of the child to adjust itself in vibration more harmoniously with the name chosen, insuring for the incoming ego an easier life in which so much adjustment is not needed.

CHAPTER IX

HARMONIOUS ASSOCIATION

PERHAPS the most severe of life's initiations are handed to us over the line of association, for it is difficult to find any individual who cannot recall that at some stage of their life they have allowed themselves to become linked in important relationships which have proved to be productive of disagreeable experiences.

In many instances a separation from these relationships has been effected and in the degree that many important lessons were learned we can label the chapter " good."

Yet again, there are still many individuals who remain in these unsatisfactory relationships, passing up day by day, to the best of their understanding, the proofs of endurance which will claim their release.

[69]

Experience is a hard master if a thorough one, but the object of the enlightened truths which are slowly forcing their way through the religious education of our day, is the promise that the time is not far distant when all will learn their human lessons by the easier, if more rapid way of transmutation or the true understanding of the experiences with which the life is linked and the wisdom which will make for conscious choice for the future.

To help this time forward is one of the aims of Numerology, which teaches many laws for selection in human association which are just as definite and simple as those which it offers for the interpretation of the mystery of the individual Self, and of which the following are examples.

We have found from the previous chapters that the numbers of the Ideality, Expression and PATH OF LIFE are the most important.

Therefore, to find the planes of complete harmony and happiness in all associations, it is only necessary to make a comparison of these vibrations in our own and another's Number-scope.

Every day we meet individuals to whom we are immediately drawn by a force which although hard for our human minds to analyze, is nevertheless above the consideration of sex, worldly position, class or creed; in other words, they are friends before we hardly realize the fact that they are " recent acquaintances."

A comparison of our numbers would show that the " Expressions " (the number we obtain from the addition of the vowels and consonants in the baptismal name) are identical.

The new civilization fundamental of " Life in the Long Run," applied through vibration, shows these individuals as companions of a former life when the vibration which is now expressed by both was being experienced or learned as the number of The Path of Life.

It is not always that such individuals

whom we meet thus, become really important to us by closer relationship of love, marriage or business; because the harmony which we feel is more the result of the past than a certainty of the present or promise for the future, and is sufficient only to insure good fellowship and to help us recognize an harmonious friend.

For the deeper associations, the individuals with whom we can obtain lasting harmony, must have vibrations which are attuned to our Ideality—our inner nature; we can prove this is so by a comparison of our own Ideality number with that of any individual who we know is really in sympathy with our deeper thoughts, visions and ideals and has proved their willingness to stand with us for their development, apart from how opposite to our expression this individual may be, or how far removed from our personal life.

It is in Ideality, therefore, that the real plane of *understanding* in love, marriage and business lies; and complete happiness and confidence in either association is impossible unless harmony in this vibration obtains.

There are many associations contracted by parties whose Ideality numbers are not the same, but in these instances it is more the plane of tolerance than of complete understanding and a certain kind of compromising harmony can be maintained by each individual refraining from the display of the deeper nature with all its personal visionings, hopes and ideals. The ideals of those finding themselves in such relationships and not knowing the law of vibration, are daily crucified and sacrificed upon the altar of misunderstanding and resistance, whereas a knowledge of such truths, and what is more important, their discovery when the association is young, can, and does bring happiness upon the planes of harmony that caused the association to be born in the first place.

In business partnerships, the Ideality numbers play again as important a part, for the true success of the relationship here, rests with each individual who represents the organization, having the same interests at heart.

" The house divided against itself " that cannot stand, is the business that has two or more partners who, however much agreement or distinct individual ability they may show in expression, misunderstand the common ideal, or are grinding the personal axe. This is invariably the case when the numbers of the individual Idealities are opposite in value.

When through a little practice with the methods suggested, we are able for ourselves to find the vibrations of a full baptismal name, and meet with a person whose Expression number is our own Path of Life number, we can know that here is an individual who, however casually met, will occupy an important association in our life; because *all things,* including persons, that vibrate to our Path of Life number are expressing on their own plane the lesson

[74]

we have come to learn and therefore stand in the relation of our greatest teachers, whether they themselves realize it or not.

The associations thus formed as a result of this attraction, although always important are not always productive of the most complete harmony, but a comparison again of the numbers of the individual Idealities, will forecast accurately in such cases how the relationship will develop.

When we meet such individuals who are vibrating in " Expression " to our " Path of Life," it is difficult for us to be content with the lighter associations. It is therefore only the knowledge of where the promise of lasting harmony can be found that when we find " Ideality " vibrations opposite in value that we can assert our knowledge and choose to avoid the closer partnership which is being forced upon us.

Inharmony is found where one "Ideality" is an odd number and the other an even.

Harmony, where both " Idealities " are the same number.

[75]

CHAPTER X

CHOOSING A LIFE'S WORK

IT is well known that the subject of choosing a vocation is a world-wide problem. At some time or another it has claimed the attention of the head of every family for one or more of its members commencing the climb toward personal achievement.

Advice upon this problem is attempted by every science and teacher claiming to possess knowledge in advance of the general understanding of the average person and still there are thousands who have never been guided, thousands who have been guided wrongly, and millions of failures every year.

We have read " Success is the product of success methods and failure the product of failure methods."

There are some failure methods, so fine, however, that it is only the trained psychologist who can discern and adjust them, and although they are all productive of destruction they are lost beside the greatest of all failure methods which it hardly needs a psychologist to observe, viz.: the individual, doing the wrong work, in the wrong way, in the wrong place.

It is this failure or its varying degrees, that Numerology, or the Science of Numbers, can adjust into harmony and which should receive the personal attention of every individual engaged in anything at all, today.

It is not always possible or easy to live our lives by psychology, because the laws which are recommended by the science are new to the race understanding; but it is an hopeless attempt for the one who is unfamiliar with the first psychiatry of all —the Psychology of the Self.

The mind of man, the master mind of the Universe, containing the power to

[77]

operate and control every law of the earth plane, is such an adjustable thing that a suggestion for better understanding coming from an outside source can be received, accepted and acted upon.

It is of this faculty that " efficiency " experts who work with objective methods take advantage and develop, so that in time an individual can be taught to disregard his own opinion and become an automaton with senses trained to detect the slightest error in his own or another's way of doing things.

Such work is good but not best, neither does it make for true efficiency which is, after all, only conscious subjective and objective unity with the thing we do.

We have seen that every mind is a storehouse of knowledge, gained from certain experience in many lines of expression included sometime, somewhere. This knowledge is recorded in the individuality and personality of the present life; it can be read by numerous signs and symbols set

[78]

in the form and it is hidden in every letter of the name.

We have no patience with the man, who having a balance in the bank, is starving upon half a loaf and denying himself the necessities of life. Yet day after day around us, ninety per cent of men and women, feeling dimly the consciousness of certain ability within themselves, never even consult the cosmic pass-book of the Self, to unfold the treasures accumulated, but think to attain success by favoring systems which train them to make the daily half loaf of objective doing, go the farthest.

We do not need to spend time and money developing man's efficiency by methods that take into account what he can be *made* to do before what he *can* do.

With knowledge you can graft a pear and apple tree, but it is not natural law; with the same knowledge you can graft the expression of a machinist on to the mind of an artist, without having the wisdom to see that the consciousness of the artist will not accept and still continues to vibrate in its own current.

Efficiency grafting is good knowledge and so is the gardener's kind; they both show a step in progress; but they are less than the wisdom that considers the law of evolution.

It is true that by such methods, twenty-five per cent efficiency is unfolded into fifty or even seventy-five per cent; but the efficiency shoe pinches between this point and the one hundred mark. You cannot walk with it into the place where success sits and feel comfortable and certain—it is made on the wrong last.

On every plane of earth's expression the law of usefulness exists, but to be successful, each unit must be scientifically related to its work in life.

Individuality is a great factor in the success of the individual and this factor is only seen where the work expresses the consciousness of its doer and is the active result of something deeper than training.

Our work in life should be an inborn habit, not a trick that we have acquired.

Even when we have found our individuality we have one other obstacle to remove from the path of success and this is the old idea of competition.

The old world leaves its cradle to enter the game, trained to move on the board of life to the advantage of himself and the temporary disadvantage of those engaged in apparently the same line of expression. The new world enters the race with all thought, energy and action, concentrated around himself and his own point of expression, not because he is selfish or even egotistical, but because he knows that he occupies a niche in life which, as he understands better, will hold all the success he needs and such success as only he himself can ever take away.

Competition is like the dummy race-horses which for a penny can be manipulated over the track of a glass-covered machine. The red and the green advance alternately, the race is short and sharp, the result—wrist-ache for the players and the horses back at first position. It is the enemy of physical fitness, youth, temper and ideals and the friend of breakdown, insanity, old age and despondency.

The only individuals to whom competition is a truth are they who are being called successes and even complimented for their efficiency, who in their heart know that they are failures because they stand self-revealed through two selves: one trained to the minute to conform to objective laws of the work in which they are engaged, and the other, wishing and building perhaps for some other thing which the more expresses them.

These are they who always need the vacations to gather together enough energy to resume their necessary efforts to hold on to something which is not theirs, to dodge the reality of competition and to cover up from the world and their associates the insecurity of their position. They do not succeed in deceiving themselves, but knowing not how to help themselves, they persist year in and year out, until perhaps through the study of sciences that can accomplish their freedom, or just through the resistance they have offered to life, they are lifted out where they can make anew the situations of their life.

CHAPTER XI

WHAT AND HOW

THE purpose of this book is to give practical aid in seeking objective and subjective success, first in discovering that quality which tells *what* we are gifted to do and secondly in showing how we can get this gift the more easily out into expression.

Numerology has some very definite and well-defined laws for this purpose, just as clear and accurate when skillfully applied as the figures which it uses in interpretation.

It believes that both the *what* and the *how* of an individual's life work are contained in the letters and numbers of the full baptismal name which we dealt with in Chapter III as telling the individual's character.

The number that corresponds with the " Ideality " shows what effort we are capable of putting our whole selves into and it is from the quality of this vibration according to the following table that we can decide which aspect of business, religion, art, etc., we can adopt upon which to build up the structure of our life's work.

IDEALITY TABLE

Ideality No.
1. CREATIVE—Mental.
2. CONSTRUCTIVE—Mental and physical.
3. EXPRESSIVE—Inspirational.
4. TECHNICAL—Mental or physical.
5. SCIENTIFIC—Inspirational.
6. EDUCATIONAL—Mental.
7. THEORETICAL—Inspirational.
8. COMMERCIAL—Mental.
9. ARTISTIC—Inspirational.

The numbers 1, 3, 5, 7, 8, 9 in Ideality give the desire and the ability to work in all occupations which their relative " Expressions " may decide, in individual freedom; this can be taken advantage of providing the Path of Life vibrations as found

in Chapter VII are in harmony with the
" Expression."

On the other hand, Idealities of 2, 4, 6,
do not have to claim individual effort in
the occupation for which their " Expression " may suit them unless the Path of
Life vibration in conjunction with them
is of the 1, 3, 5, 7, 8, 9 vibrations.

For example, we will take an illustration of an Ideality of 7 which is the theoretical inspirational quality desiring and
having ability for individual effort. In
choosing a successful work for such an individual we would have to satisfy ourselves
that in any particular occupation which
his " Expression " might decide, he had
the opportunity to express his theories
which would probably be of a literary or
religious nature.

When we have claimed conformity with
that inner quality, seen from the vibration
of " Ideality," the next step is to find the
objective channel or occupation through
which it can be developed and expressed to

conform with the requirements of our modern world.

The "Expression" vibration of the individual decides this very necessary question and tells whether business, art, commerce, etc., should receive our efforts.

The following table gives the zone of each Expression number and a few of the vocations which agree with them and it is a simple matter for each reader to determine to which zone any particular occupation which we have no room to enumerate here, but which he favors for adoption, conforms.

Expression No.
1. CREATION—System. Analysis. Invention.
2. CONSTRUCTION—Diplomacy. Politics.
3. PERSONAL EXPRESSION—Individual art. Adornment. Criticism.
4. MATERIAL CONSTRUCTION — Technicality. Planning. Building.
5. SCIENCE—Salesmanship. Experimenting. Pioneering. Advertising.
6. EDUCATION—Domesticity. Responsibility. Teaching.
7. THEORY—Literature. Religion.
8. COMMERCE—Organization. Management. Valuation. Direction.
9. UNIVERSAL EXPRESSION—Art. Entertainment. Philanthropy. Music. Healing.

We can cite an illustration of the combination of the vibration of Ideality and Expression in the choice of a vocation as follows:

Ideality 7, Expression 1=Subjective, theoretical inspirational ideals expressed through a creative mental occupation—for example, literature.

Again, an individual with Ideality 5 and Expression 4 should engage in a physical, technical occupation that expressed his scientific inspirational ideality; example—a surgeon.

Another individual with Expression 9 and Ideality 8 could choose an occupation of Universal Expression, art, entertainment, etc., so long as the commercial mental ideals were revealed through its expression and the common mistake in such a combination, that of attempting to work solely as the artist, was not made.

Remember that there are just nine numbers or vibrations to deal with and by knowing the nature of any occupation and find-

'ing the numbers of your Ideality and Expression it is quickly seen where and how a correct choice can be made to insure the perfect combination between the special quality of the Ideality with the ability of the Expression.

It will be readily understood that the lack of perfect understanding of these two distinct vibrations causes a great deal of ill adjustment; but that understood, they are the infallible means of harmony between what we desire to do and how we can actually do it.

The combination of artist and business man, for instance, is not a rare one, but how to develop such dual ability into harmonious success and usefulness is a neglected part of the world's education.

CHAPTER XII

COMPLETE ADJUSTMENT

IN order to have complete success, it is not even enough that individuals should do the work for which they are fitted according as we have seen to the perfect combination of Ideality and Expression vibration; but also, that they should develop this work to the people who will appreciate them and their efforts and in the environment which helps them to increase their usefulness and happiness and fulfills the purpose of their life.

The almost complete ignorance of how to decide this very natural law, by the sciences which are better known to the world as competent to choose vocations, is a great factor in the dissatisfaction of individuals with their positions in life and often the main cause which keeps them out of the recognition which their development really merits.

Many times a man who has successfully worked for an organization, doing work for which he is well fitted, is taken, by the nature of his firm's business, all over the country and brought into relation with a certain class of individuals. A time comes perhaps when this man feels that he would like to set up for himself in the same line of business, but by the nature of his own plans he eliminates, accidentally perhaps, the class of individuals to whom he has formerly expressed, or puts himself into positions that cannot include the extensive travel which his former position made necessary.

He finds after a short while that he cannot make a success of his own venture, and is compelled to work again in association which he does not prefer. He many times condemns his own lack of ability for his failure, or perhaps calls it "bad luck," when the law of vibration will and does show him that the whole reason was that he did not know that a certain class of individuals, conditions, and environment were more necessary to his success than another.

For another illustration, we can consider the case of two men, both perfect salesmen, trained and capable of promoting business in the same organization.

According to a science of character analysis we place these two men in almost identical positions with some big house having two vacancies in their retail section. We allow only in our choice for the little difference in the two temperaments.

We have assured ourselves previously that both are capable of that quality of salesmanship which can deal with the many different classes of buyers that will come in for attention and we are at first gratified to see that each man shows satisfactory returns.

In a little while, however, it is observed that one of these two men is showing fatigue, finding his work more irksome and feeling it more difficult each week to keep up in his sales and general attentiveness with his companion.

Perhaps he is told that he has been working too hard and an opportunity to rest is gladly afforded, but such an act only seems to delay the day when he feels unable to continue his work and loses finally the appreciation of his talent which his employers were at first so ready to acknowledge.

What has happened? He cannot have lost his usefulness as a salesman, because all the laws of character analysis have declared that he is fitted for the work. No, he should not do other work; for his talent still remains in the line in which he has been engaged, simply waiting for the recognition that he has been developing it in the *wrong environment.* He has been rowing up instead of down the stream of his usefulness. He is fit, trained to the minute to control the craft in which he has been sailing, but just unaware that there was any particular river on which to launch it that led more directly than another to the sea of success.

Each of these two men had minds productive of thoughts which were real things capable of making success or failure. The first found the right environment in which his set of thoughts about himself and his work could be unfolded and developed into harmonious growth, and the other found the atmosphere to which he was not attuned and could not develop happiness or even energy to perform the tasks for which he was really fitted.

Outside in the big world perhaps, doing the same work but with a different class of conditions and individuals, where he could learn to break new ground day by day and week by week, he could have unfolded his talents, instead of having suppressed them, until he found a consciousness of his place in the sun as great as that of his companion.

It is here that we apply the understanding of our Path of Life vibration as found in Chapter VII, as this dictates just the kind of people who can appreciate us the most, just the atmosphere in which we should express ourselves and just the conditions that must be conformed with even in the work for which our temperament and ability have fitted us, if we would have that " four-square " feeling to life, which is superior to limitation or the circumstances of the moment.

" Where? " and " To whom? " then, are just as important questions as " What can I do? " and " How can I do it? "

CHAPTER XIII

WHERE AND TO WHOM

WE have seen that the existence of the Path of Life vibration is the reason why so many individuals are linked with people, conditions and situations which they do not understand and so often make the mistake of resisting.

All the while there remain these people, conditions and situations with which our lack of understanding is developing us out of harmony, just so long is it logically to be expected that our complete success will keep away from us, even though we may have found the work we love and are fitted to accomplish.

Each individual is living for something higher than to express continually the likes and understandings of his own nature and reject all expressions that do not conform to his ideals.

To the one who knows this, the very feeling of dislike is a signal, that here is something that he does not understand and while he cannot readily accept such expressions as his own, yet realizing that there is "good in everything," he inquires of science how he can make the adjustment to bring this good to the surface, and whether it is an expression which he needs to include for his perfect success in this life.

No matter what occupation one might he fitted for, if the Path of Life number was 6, he would have to express to the great mass of people coming in the domestic, active and responsible zone and in order to gain complete success, to comply in the nature of his expression with such conditions as these individuals would demand and appreciate.

The following example is sufficient to

prove the value of the adjustment which Numerology attempts.

A young woman possessing marked artistic, dramatic and musical abilities was trained for a number of years until she was declared proficient to enter the operatic stage. Everyone, including professionals, remarked upon the quality of her work— but that was all, usually. The opportunities she received never amounted to anything worth while. She came to the Author one day with the question, " What is the matter with me? "

There was never anything the matter with her or her ability as an artist; she had simply developed this ability entirely as dictated by her high ideals which were fostered by her parents; and in utter ignorance that there was a special field of endeavor waiting for her, she chose an expression that only appealed to the minority.

A glance at her Path of Life vibration revealed the fact that the masses and not the classes were waiting for her revelation, ready to hand her the success which she deserved.

This lady acted upon the advice that was given her; took a course of instruction in work that could reveal her ideal the more clearly to those individuals whom she was in this life to inspire and today is on the way to occupy one of the first places among motion picture players. She sees success ahead and is not dissatisfied with the expression of her ideal.

What an understanding for so many with business abilities even, trained in definite assured lines, who have never gained any appreciable measure of success, to know that it may all be that they are appealing to a class of individuals and in an atmosphere dictated it is true by their own likes and dislikes, but where they and the quality of their work will never be appreciated; or perhaps they have developed their talents along lines that can never bring the fullest measure of success on the material plane.

Below is a summary of the vibrations 1 to 9 as they are to be interpreted when they appear as the Path of Life vibration. They tell the zones in which and the class of people to whom we have to express that work which we have chosen as our own.

1. Should work unassociated with others, as pioneers; or if associated, endeavor to appeal to individuals rather than to masses, developing individuality. Make work understandable to creative, mental individuals.

2. Should work associated with others, appealing to the masses rather than individuals, developing collection and experience in dealing with the finer side of materiality and with less developed individuals.

3. Should work unassociated with others, appealing to individuals rather than the masses, developing perfected personal expression, making the individual work ac-

ceptable to social, inspirational and artistic individuals.

4. Should work in association rather than unassociated, appealing to the masses rather than to individuals; developing construction, order, arrangement.

5. Should work unassociated with others, appealing to scientific, resourceful, inventive individuals and those who are expressing personal freedom, rather than to the masses.

6. Should work in association with others, appealing to the domestic, responsible masses rather than to individuals. Developing usefulness.

7. Should work unassociated with others, appealing to individuals that are attracted to theories, rather than the masses. Developing study and reflection.

8. Can work either in association or organization or unassociated; should appeal to both masses and individuals of the commercial and intellectual zones. Developing material perfection.

[101]

9. Can work either in association, or unassociated; appealing to both masses and individuals of the artistic, emotional and inspirational type. Developing complete expression.

CHAPTER XIV

CONCLUSION

ALL nature is scientific. It expresses in order by divine law and there is nothing of the waste of energy that is found to be the cause of such ill adjustment on the human plane.

One individual has an ideal, but measuring himself and it by the environment and the minds around him, he surrenders it more or less as an impossibility for him.

Another is attracted to adopt a certain vocation because as he has seen others express it, it is agreeable to him; he finds however that the ideal back of this expression is foreign to him as he has learned to interpret himself.

Yet another is allowing his likes and

dislikes to dictate the plane upon which he is expressing his ideal and ability and day by day he is resisting true Opportunity, because he does not approve of the style of her dress.

In all these very human instances there is that separating, isolating influence that will always make success an uncertainty and the only way to eliminate the misunderstanding is to get back to order—God's first law in the Universe.

The great notions of a little child are only developed and made possible through its initial lessons of A, B, C, and 1, 2, 3, and in the same way, our own great notions about ourselves and success are only made possible by the understanding of the A, B, C, of ourselves and our relation to life.

"Except ye become as a little child . . ." has many interpretations; but certainly, except we use the little child's first principle of mathematics, we can never tabulate accurately the zone of our ideals, the channel through which they should be expressed, or decide through figures " that cannot lie " the Path of Life that leads to completeness.

CPSIA information can be obtained at www.ICGtesting.com
Printed in the USA
LVOW09s1711070415

433627LV00006B/681/P